Roald Dahl
Rhyme Stew

Illustrations by Quentin Blake

JONATHAN CAPE
LONDON

For Liccy

First published 1989
Reprinted 1989 (four times), 1996, 1998
Text © 1989 Felicity Dahl and the other
Executors of the Estate of Roald Dahl
Illustrations © Quentin Blake 1989

Roald Dahl and Quentin Blake have asserted
their right under the Copyright, Designs and
Patents Act 1988 to be identified as the author
and illustrator of this work

Jonathan Cape Limited
Random House, 20 Vauxhall Bridge Road,
London SW1V 2SA

Random House UK Limited Reg. No. 954009

A CIP catalogue record for this book is
available from the British Library

ISBN 0-224-02660-7

Printed in China

Contents

Dick Whittington and His Cat

Dick Whittington had oft been told
That London's streets were paved with gold.
"We'd better have a look at that,"
He murmured to his faithful cat.
And finally they made it there
And finished up in Berkeley Square.
So far so good, but Dicky knew
That he must find some work to do.
Imagine, if you can, his joy
At being made the pantry-boy
To Lord and Lady Hellespont!
What more could any young lad want?
His Lordship's house was huge and warm,
Each footman wore a uniform,
Rich carpets lay on all the floors,
And big brass door-knobs on the doors.
Why, Whittington had never seen
A house so marvellously clean,
Although, regrettably, his cat
Soon did some things to alter that.

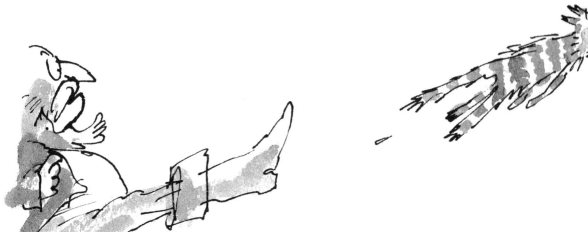

His Lordship kicked the cat so hard
It landed in a neighbour's yard,
But still each morning on the floor
It did what it had done before.
His Lordship shouted, "Fetch my gun!
I'll nail the blighter on the run!
Call up the beaters! Flush him out!
I know he's somewhere hereabout!"

It is a fact that wealthy men
Do love to shoot things now and then.
They shoot at partridge, pheasant, grouse,
Though not so much *inside* the house.
But now His Lordship stalks the brute
With gun in hand, prepared to shoot.
He crouches down behind a chair.
Ah-ha! What's moving over there?
Of course the poor sap couldn't know
His wife was on the portico,
Locked in a passionate embrace
With second footman, Albert Grace.
The gun goes off, *bang-bang*, *boom-boom*!
The noise explodes around the room.
You should have seen the lady jump
As grapeshot struck her in the rump,

And in the kitchen, washing up,
Dick jumps and breaks a precious cup.
This is a crime no decent cook
Could bring herself to overlook.
This cook, a brawny powerful wench,
Put Whittington across the bench
And systematically began
To beat him with a frying-pan
Which she had very quickly got
From off the stove, all sizzling hot.

Poor Whittington, his rump aflame,
At last escapes the fearsome dame
And runs outside across the street,
Clutching his steaming smoking seat.
The cat, now very frightened, said,
"Let's beat it quick before we're dead."
At that point, with an angry shout
Her Ladyship comes flying out.
(Although indeed she had been shot,
It wasn't in a vital spot.)
She yells, "I'm on the run as well!
Old Hellespont can go to hell!"
Just then, a peal of bells rings out.
Each bell begins to sing and shout,
And Dick could quite distinctly hear
A message coming through the air.
He actually could hear his name!
He heard the Bells of Bow proclaim –

> *Turn again, Whittington,*
> *Thou worthy citizen,*
> *Turn again, Whittington,*
> *Lord Mayor of London*!

"Lord Mayor of London!" cries the cat.
"I've never heard such rot as that!"
Her Ladyship butts in and yells,
"The cat is right! That's not the *bells*!

Bow church has got a crazy vicar,
A famous and fantastic tricker,
A disco king, a hi-fi buff,
A whizz on electronic stuff.
He's rigged up speakers in the steeple
To fool dim-witted country people.
Listen, you poor misguided youth,
In London no one tells the truth!"
She looks at Dick. Dick looks at her.
She smiles and says, "My dear sir,
I must say I prefer your face
To second footman, Albert Grace.
I think we'd make a nifty team,
With me the strawberries, you the cream."

The cat cries, "Dick, you do not want
To fool with Lady Hellespont!
These females from the upper-classes
Spend their lives in making passes!"
At this point, with a mighty roar,
Lord Hellespont bursts through the door.
He sees his wife. He lifts his gun.
The lady screams and starts to run.
Once more, with a colossal thump,
The grapeshot strikes her in the rump.
"Oh gosh!" Dick cries. "I do declare
That no one's bum seems safe in here!"

The furious red-faced lady stands
Clutching her bottom in her hands,
And shouts, "You quite deliberately
Pointed that filthy gun at me!"
He cries, "I aimed it at the cat."
The lady shouts, "The cat my hat!
You don't think I'm believing that!"
"Oh yes, you must!" His Lordship cries,
Blinking his crafty boozy eyes.
"I simply cannot be to blame
Because *all cats* look much the same."
The cat cried, "That's a vicious slur!
How dare you say I look like *her*!"

Now Whittington pulls out his sword
And runs it through the noble Lord,
Shouting, "Gadzooks! Hooray! There passes
One member of the upper-classes!"

Her ladyship leaps high with joy
And cries, "Well done, my scrumptious boy!
The old goat's clobbered once for all!
Now you and I can have a ball!"
The cat shouts, "Dick, do not succumb
To blandishments from that old crumb!
And by the way, the man who told
That London's streets were paved with gold
Was telling dreadful porky-pies."
(That's cockney rhyming-slang for lies.)
The cat went on, "To me it seems
These streets are paved with rotten dreams.
Come home, my boy, without more fuss.
This lousy town's no place for us."
Dick says, "You're right," then sighs and mumbles,
"Well well, that's how the cookie crumbles."

St Ives

As I was going to St Ives
I met a man with seven wives.
Said he, "I think it's much more fun
Than getting stuck with only one."

16

A Hand in the Bird

I'm a maiden who is forty,
And a maiden I shall stay.
There are some who call me haughty,
But I care not what they say.

I was running the tombola
At our church bazaar today,
And doing it with gusto
In my usual jolly way...

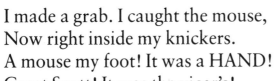

When suddenly, I knew not why,
There came a funny feeling
Of something *crawling up my thigh*!
I nearly hit the ceiling!

A mouse! I thought. How foul! How mean!
How exquisitely tickly!
Quite soon I know I'm going to scream.
I've got to catch it quickly.

I made a grab. I caught the mouse,
Now right inside my knickers.
A mouse my foot! It was a HAND!
Great Scott! It was the vicar's!

The Tortoise and the Hare

The Tortoise long ago had learned
(So far as eating was concerned)
That nothing in the world could match
Old Mister Roach's cabbage-patch.
Potatoes, lettuce, cabbage, peas
Could all be had with perfect ease
(Provided you had first checked out
That Mister Roach was not about.)
The Tortoise had for very long
Enjoyed this lovely restaurant,
But all at once – Oh, shame! Disgrace!
A ghastly thing was taking place!
That horrid Hare began to poach
The sacred land of Mister Roach.
And worst of all, the Hare got rid
Of far more than the Tortoise did.
With beans he'd eat up every one
Before the Tortoise had begun!
The carrots all were out of sight
Before poor Torty had one bite!
The lettuce, succulent and green,
Was suddenly no longer seen!
And so the Tortoise now began
To hatch a very subtle plan.

He came across the Hare at dawn
Demolishing a row of corn,
And said to him, "Would you agree
To have a sporting bet with me?
I don't believe I've ever met
A hare who could refuse a bet."
Hare said, "I must admit I play
The horses almost every day."
The Tortoise said, "I'm betting you
I'd win a race between us two."
"You're round the twist!" the Hare cried out.
"You're bonkersville! You're up the spout!
Why, I could run to Equador
Before you'd even crossed the floor!

I'd run from here to Cowdenbeath
Before you'd even brushed your teeth!
I'd run to Poole and Beachy Head
Before you're hardly out of bed!
Don't talk to me of how to run!
A hare can outpace anyone!"
The Tortoise said, "Although you're fast
I'm betting you you'll come in last.
And by the way, you might recall
Pride always comes before a fall."
The Hare was so convulsed with scorn
He nearly choked upon his corn.
He gagged and coughed, but when he spake
He cried, "You're on! So what's the stake?"
The Tortoise after saying, "Well,"
Produced from underneath his shell
A pen, a contract and a seal
And then began to read the deal:
"If I do lose I hereby swear
That I will nevermore go near
Or take the tiniest of nibbles
From Mister Roach's vegitibbles."
The Hare considered for a while,
Then answered with a knowing smile,
"That all seems eminently fair,"
And signed it with a flourish – *Hare.*
The Hare was later heard to say
Quite loudly, in a scornful way,
"Well Torty, when this race is run,
When you have lost and I have won,
I don't know where you'll go to dine,
But that is no concern of mine."

The Tortoise now went on to call
On Mister Rat at evenfall,
And found him in his workshop where
The Rat was trying to repair
A fascinatingly bizarre
Bright saffron-yellow motor-car.
The Rat was famous everywhere
As being a brilliant engineer,
But just like all the ratty clan
He was a crafty business man
And well-nigh guaranteed to rob
His customers on every job.
"Hello, old Rat," the Tortoise cries,
Regarding him through scaly eyes.
"I've come along tonight to ask
About a highly secret task."

Rat, slowly putting down his spanner,
Assumed a sympathetic manner.
"My dear old Torty," he declared,
"Now if you want your car repaired..."
"No, no!" the Tortoise cried. "You're wrong.
Now here's the burden of my song."
He then explained with skill and flair
The details of his bet with Hare.
The Rat said, "Ho! I do believe
There's something fishy up your sleeve.
It's obvious if the race was fair
You'd have no chance against the Hare.
In fact, however much you cheat,
You'll never never never beat
That speedy Hare. You are a dope
To think you have the slightest hope."
The Tortoise said, "There is, old Rat,
More ways than one to skin a cat."
Rat cried, "Be sensible, old man!
Look, even if I were to ram
A red-hot poker up your blaster,
You wouldn't travel any faster."
"Hold it!" the Tortoise cried. "My wheeze,
And listen carefully if you please,
My brilliant wonderful idea
Is that you build for me right here
A little four-wheeled motor-car
That travels fast and very far,
Which you can screw beneath my shell
In such a way no man can tell,
Not even bright-eyed Mister Hare,
That I've got anything down there.

I'll wave my legs and off I'll go
And Mister Hare will never know
What's giving me this wondrous power
To run at sixty miles an hour.
Oh Rat, I know you'll do it right –
The little wheels just out of sight,
The engine tucked away as well,
All hidden underneath my shell!"
The Rat was stunned. He stretched his eyes,
He stood and shouted with surprise,
"By gum, I never would have guessed
An ancient bird like you possessed
Such genius in your upper storey!
This has to be your path to glory!
I'll do the job this very night
Provided that the price is right."
"How much? How much?" the Tortoise cried.
"That all depends," the Rat replied,
"Which motor you require on board,
A Rolls, a Bentley or a Ford?"
"The fastest one!" the Tortoise said.
"I want a racing thoroughbred!"
The deal was struck, arrangements made
And willingly the Tortoise paid.

As soon as Rat was all alone
He tiptoed to the telephone
And asked to speak to Mister Hare,
And said, "Hello, it's Ratty here."
The Hare said, "Hello Rat, what's new?
And how are things tonight with you?"
Rat answered, "Would you pay a lot
To hear about an evil plot?
Would you, for instance, give your shirt
To know who's going to do you dirt?"
There was a silence on the line,
Then Hare cried, "Who's the rotten swine?
Come on now, Ratty, tell me true!
You know I'd do the same for you!"
The Rat said, very soft and sly,
"No go, old man. Goodbye, goodbye."
"Wait! Wait!" cried Hare. "Don't go away!
How much d'you want? I'll pay! I'll pay!"
And so once more old Ratty made
A very advantageous trade,
And after he had got his fee
He told of Torty's villainy.
The Hare jumped up and down and cried,
"That's cheating! He's disqualified!"
The Rat, with nauseating joy,
Said, "Hate to tell you this, old boy,
Your contract simply says you race,
The two of you, from place to place.
It doesn't ban the clever use
Of engines giving extra juice."
"I'm cooked!" the Hare yelled out. "I'm done!
I'll lose my favourite restaurant!"

The Rat said, slimier than ever,
"Are you forgetting rats are clever?
I'm sure arrangements could be made
Provided *extra* cash is paid.
I could for instance guarantee,
In token of this extra fee,
That irrespective of how fast
The Tortoise goes, you won't be last.
I'd see that all his tyres go flat,
I'd guarantee it," said the Rat.
"How much, how much?" the other cried.
"An awful lot," the Rat replied.
The Hare now paid a second bill,
And Dirty Rat got richer still.

This thrilling epoch-making race
Was by agreement taking place
Along the road beneath the hill
To finish by the barley-mill.
The Rat meanwhile had tipped a load
Of spiky nails across the road,
Then hid himself, when that was done,
Behind the hedge to see the fun.

Spectators all along the way
Had come to watch and shout hooray,
The field-mice, weasels, hedgehogs, stoats
And rabbits in their furry coats
All lined the route and waved their flags
And picnicked out of paper-bags.
An ancient fox who ran the show
Yelled out, "Get ready! Steady! Go!"
Now Torty gunned his great machine
And off he went in clouds of steam,
And soon because of all that power
Was doing fifty miles an hour.

Each time he had to change a gear,
Black smoke came belching from his rear.
Each time he had to use the brake,
His shell began to creak and shake.
But oh, it was a wondrous thing
To see a tortoise on the wing.
"I'm going to win with lengths to spare!"
The Tortoise yelled to Mister Hare.
"Oh no you're not!" the Hare replied,
"For I've got Ratty on my side!"
And just a moment after that
All four of Torty's tyres went flat.

He had to stop. He had no choice,
And Hare, in an exultant voice,
Cried out, "Well, that's the end of you!
Stand back! Stand back! I'm coming through!"
The Hare forgot that just ahead
Lay all the nails that Rat had spread.
The spiky things were everywhere
And silly foolish Mister Hare
Had spikes in every foot and toe!
He couldn't run! He couldn't go!

He shouted, "I can run no more!
We'll have to call the race a draw."
The Tortoise, all his tyres flat,
Said sadly, "I agree to that."
Meanwhile the dirty Mister Rat
Went home and counted all his pay.
He'd had a profitable day.
So just remember if you can,
Don't tangle with a business man.
It doesn't matter who you choose,
They always win, we always lose.
If you were here and I was there,
If you were Tortoise, I was Hare,
We'd both get diddled in the end
By people like our Ratty friend.

The Price of Debauchery

My mother said, "There are no joys
In ever kissing silly boys.
Just one small *kiss* and one small squeeze
Can land you with some foul disease."

"But Mum, d'you mean from just a *kiss*?"

"You know quite well my meaning, miss."

Last week when coming home from school
I clean forgot Mum's golden rule.
I let Tom Young, that handsome louse,
Steal one small kiss behind my house.

Oh, woe is me! I've paid the price!
I should have listened to advice.
My mum was right one hundredfold!
I've caught Tom's horrid runny cold!

Physical Training

Our gym-instructress, Miss McPhee,
When gym was over, said to me,
"Stay on, Bill Smith, I'll teach you things.
I'll make you better on the rings,
And after that let's reinforce
Your work upon the vaulting horse."
I stayed behind. She shut the door.
She'd never been so kind before.
She said, "So you can get it right
I'll have to hold you very tight."
She held me here, she held me there,
By gum, she held me everywhere.
She kindly taught me, after that,
To wrestle with her on the mat.
Oh! gosh, the things she taught to me,
Our gym-instructress, Miss McPhee!

The Emperor's New Clothes

The Royal Tailor, Mister Ho,
Had premises on Savile Row,
And thence the King would make his way
At least a dozen times a day.
His passion was for gorgeous suits
And sumptuous cloaks and fur-lined boots
And brilliant waistcoats lined in red,
Hand-sewn with gold and silver thread.
Within the Palace things were grand,
With valets everywhere on hand
To hang the clothes and clean and press
And help the crazy King to dress.
But clothes are very dangerous things,
Especially for wealthy kings.
This King had gone to pot so fast,
His clothes came first, his people last.
One valet who was seen to leave
A spot of gravy on a sleeve
Was hung from rafters by his hair
And left forever dangling there.
Another who had failed to note
A fleck of dust upon a coat
Was ordered to be boiled alive,
A fate not easy to survive.
And one who left a pinch of snuff
Upon a pale-blue velvet cuff

Was minced inside a large machine
And reappeared as margarine.
Oh, what a beastly horrid King!
The people longed to do him in!
And so a dozen brainy men
Met secretly inside a den
To formulate a subtle plot
To polish off this royal clot.
Up spake the very brainiest man
Who cried, "I've got a wizard plan.
Please come with me. We all must go
To see the royal tailor, Ho.
We'll tell him very strong and true
Exactly what he's got to do."
So thus the secret plans were laid
And all arrangements quickly made.

T'was winter-time with lots of snow
And every day the King would go
To ski a bit before he dined
In ski-suits specially designed.
But even on these trips he'd stop
To go into the tailor's shop.
"O Majesty!" cried Mister Ho,
"I cannot wait to let you know
That I've contrived at last to get
From secret weavers in Tibet
A cloth so magical and fine,
So unbelievably divine,
You've never seen its like before
And never will do any more!"
The King yelled out, "I'll buy the lot!
I'll purchase every yard you've got!"
The tailor smiled and bowed his head.
"O honoured sire," he softly said,
"This marvellous magic cloth has got
Amazing ways to keep you hot,
And even when it's icy cold
You still feel warm as molten gold.
However hard the north wind blows
You still won't need your underclothes."
The King said, "If it's all that warm,
I'll have a ski-ing uniform!
I want ski-trousers and a jacket!
I don't care if it costs a packet!
Produce the cloth. I want to see
This marvellous stuff you're selling me."
The tailor, feigning great surprise,
Said, "Sire, it's here before your eyes."

The King said, "Where? Just tell me where."
"It's in my hands, o King, right here!"
The King yelled, tearing at his hair,
"Don't be an ass! There's nothing there!"
The tailor cried, "Hold on, I pray!
There's something I forgot to say!
This cloth's invisible to fools
And nincompoops and other ghouls.

For brainless men who're round the twist
This cloth does simply not exist!
But seeing how you're wise and bright,
I'm sure it glistens in your sight."
Now right on cue, exactly then,
In burst the dozen brainy men.
They shouted, "Oh, what lovely stuff!
We want some too! D'you have enough?"
Extremely calm, the tailor stands,
With nothing in his empty hands,
And says, "No, no! this gorgeous thing
Is only for my lord, the King."
The King, not wanting to admit
To being a proper royal twit
Cried out, "Oh, isn't it divine!
I want it all! It's mine! It's mine!
I want a ski-ing outfit most
So I can keep as warm as toast!"
The brainy men all cried, "Egad!
Oh, Majesty, you lucky lad!
You'll feel so cosy in the snow
With temps at zero and below!"

Next day the tailor came to fit
The costume on the royal twit.
The brainy men all went along
To see that nothing should go wrong.
The tailor said, "Strip naked, sire.
This suit's so warm you won't require
Your underclothes or pants or vest
Or even hair upon your chest."
And now the clever Mister Ho
Put on the most terrific show
Of dressing up the naked King
In nothing – not a single thing.

"That's right sir, slip your arm in there,
And now I'll zip you up right here.
Do you feel comfy? Does it fit?
Or should I take this in a bit?"
Now during this absurd charade,
And while the King was off his guard,
The brainy men, so shrewd and sly,
Had turned the central heating high.
The King, although completely bare,
With not a stitch of underwear,
Began to sweat and mop his brow,
And cried, "I do believe you now!
I feel as though I'm going to roast!
This suit will keep me warm as toast!"
The Queen, just then, came strolling through
With ladies of her retinue.
They stopped. They gasped. There stood the King
As naked as a piece of string,
As naked as a popinjay,
With not a fig-leaf in the way.

He shouted, striking up a pose,
"Behold my marvellous ski-ing clothes!
These clothes will keep me toasty-warm
In hail or sleet or snow or storm!"
Some ladies blushed and hid their eyes
And uttered little plaintive cries.
But some, it seemed, enjoyed the pleasures
Of looking at the royal treasures.
A brazen wench cried, "Oh my hat!
Hey girls, just take a look at that!"
The Queen, who'd seen it all before,
Made swiftly for the nearest door.

The King cried, "Now I'm off to ski!
You ladies want to come with me?"
They shook their heads, so off he went,
A madman off on pleasure bent.
The crazy King put on his skis,
And now, oblivious to the freeze
He shot outdoors and ski'd away,
Still naked as a popinjay.
And thus this fool, so lewd and squalid,
In half an hour was frozen solid.
And all the nation cried, "Heigh-ho!
The King's deep-frozen in the snow!"

A Little Nut-Tree

I had a little nut-tree,
Nothing would it bear.
I searched in all its branches,
But not a nut was there.

"Oh, little tree," I begged,
"Give me just a few."
The little tree looked down at me
And whispered, "Nuts to you."

The Dentist and the Crocodile

The crocodile, with cunning smile, sat in the dentist's chair.
He said, "Right here and everywhere my teeth require repair."
The dentist's face was turning white. He quivered, quaked and shook.
He muttered, "I suppose I'm going to have to take a look."
"I want you", Crocodile declared, "to do the back ones first.
The molars at the very back are easily the worst."
He opened wide his massive jaws. It was a fearsome sight –
At least three hundred pointed teeth, all sharp and shining white.
The dentist kept himself well clear. He stood two yards away.
He chose the longest probe he had to search out the decay.
"I said to do the *back ones* first!" the Crocodile called out.
"You're much too far away, dear sir, to see what you're about.
To do the back ones properly you've got to put your head
Deep down inside my great big mouth," the grinning Crocky said.
The poor old dentist wrung his hands and, weeping in despair,
He cried, "No no! I see them all extremely well from here!"

Just then, in burst a lady, in her hands a golden chain.
She cried, "Oh Croc, you naughty boy, you're playing tricks again!"
"Watch out!" the dentist shrieked and started climbing up the wall.
"He's after me! He's after you! He's going to eat us all!"
"Don't be a twit," the lady said, and flashed a gorgeous smile.
"He's harmless. He's my little pet, my lovely crocodile."

Hot and Cold

A woman who my mother knows
Came in and took off all her clothes.

Said I, not being very old,
"By golly gosh, you must be cold!"

"No, no!" she cried. "Indeed I'm not!
I'm feeling devilishly hot!"

45

Ali Baba and the Forty Thieves

A very decent Arab sport
Called Ali Baba (Al for short)
Was standing, so's to be polite,
Behind a tree and out of sight,
Performing with his normal tact
A very simple natural act.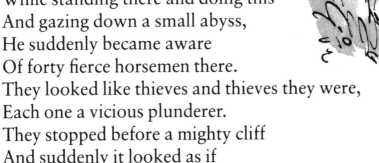
While standing there and doing this
And gazing down a small abyss,
He suddenly became aware
Of forty fierce horsemen there.
They looked like thieves and thieves they were,
Each one a vicious plunderer.
They stopped before a mighty cliff
And suddenly it looked as if
This gathering of forty thieves
Had something tricky up their sleeves.
The leader (it was surely he)
Now shouted, "Open Sesame!"
And suddenly, surprise, surprise,
In front of Ali Baba's eyes,
The mighty rockface opened wide
To show a mammoth cave inside.
Then all the forty thieves careered
Inside the cave and disappeared.
Al knew at once that he had heard
A very secret magic word.

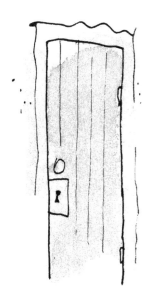

From now on he, if he was right,
Could open any door in sight.
He ran for home, he couldn't wait.
He dashed in through his garden gate
And stood, quite out of breath, before
His humble little cottage door.
He paused and counted one, two, three,
Then shouted, "Open Sesame!"
Behold! At once, this little door
Which had been firmly locked before,
Began to open very wide,
With no one helping from inside.
"It's magic!" Ali Baba screams.
"It's far beyond my wildest dreams!
I'll bet I'm able now, gee whizz,
To open any door there is!
Oh, what a power I possess!
Oh, what excitement and success!
But wait!" he said. "No need to shout!
Let's simmer down and think things out.
Young fools rush in, it's always said,
Where even angels fear to tread."
How wise. Had this been you or me,
We would have jumped up instantly
And rushed along the street point-blank
To rob the safe in Barclays Bank.
Not Ali Baba, no not he,
He wanted fun, not villainy.
And so, upon that selfsame day,
At midnight, Ali made his way
To London, which he knew quite well,
And thence into the Ritz Hotel.

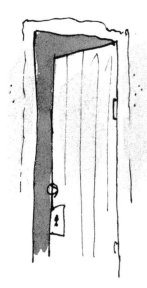

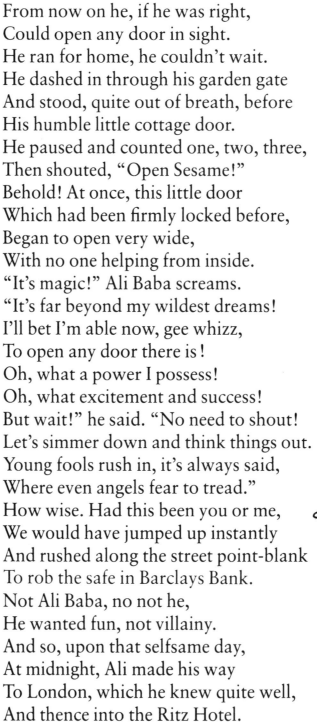

(These days a well-dressed Arab gent
In flowing robes, on pleasure bent,
Is welcomed and is treated well
In every really good hotel.)
The Ritz is truly very grand,
Perhaps the finest in the land.
The hall is full of chandeliers
And duchesses and ancient peers
And saucy women wearing jewels
And baronets and other fools.

But Ali Baba swept right through
And up the stairs and came unto
The first of all the bedroom floors
Where there were lots and lots of doors.
Slowly he walked the corridor
And as he passed each bedroom door
He took the simple liberty
Of saying "Open Sesame!"
By gosh, as each door opened wide,
He saw some funny things inside!
One man was drinking beer in bed
And one was standing on his head.
A man with a terrific snore
Was fast asleep upon the floor.
A woman in a camisole
Was dancing to some rock and roll.
In one large room, a bearded crank
Was fishing in a water-tank
With rod and line and huge delight,
And shouting out, "I've got a bite!"

A naked girl and some male freak
Were playing games of hide and seek.
While one man gobbled up a kipper,
His girl drank champagne from a slipper.

In one big bed there slept a goat,
A diamond necklace round its throat.
And in the honeymooners' suite –
What *goings-on* beneath the sheet!
As well as that, our hero saw
Some things he'd *never* seen before,
Fantastic sights both rich and rare
That no one's going to mention here.
Al could not quite believe his eyes.
"What's wrong", he gasps, "with all these guys?
The rich have most peculiar habits,
Less like humans, more like rabbits!"
And then the shouts and yells began,
From every woman, every man,
From every room, all down the floor
They yelled, "Who's opened up my door?"

They surged into the passageway
In various states of disarray,
Some naked as the day is long,
With absolutely nothing on,
The naughty girls, their virile beaus,
None of them wearing any clothes,
And then the goat came out as well,
Bringing the most appalling smell.
One man yelled out, "There's burglars here!"
And fired a pistol in the air.
A millionairess in the nude
Had to be forcibly subdued.

She cried, "My emerald bracelet's gone!
I know quite well I had it on!"
Old men, astounded at their luck,
Forgot themselves and ran amok.

Plump thighs were tweaked and bottoms pinched,
And finally a duke was lynched.
Such chaos in the corridor
No one had ever seen before!
And Ali Baba thought, By gosh,
I'm awfully glad that I'm not posh.
I wouldn't want to go round nude
Like this lot here. They're all half-stewed!
They're all completely round the bend!
I have enjoyed myself no end!
So Ali Baba, feeling swell,
Slips quietly from the Ritz Hotel.
"But wait!" he cries out as he leaves.
"What's happened to the Forty Thieves?
I clean forgot to put them in!
Oh well," he murmurs with a grin,
"Who cares? Not me. What's done is done.
I really can't please everyone."

Hey Diddle Diddle

Hey diddle diddle
We're all on the fiddle
And never get up until noon.
We only take cash
Which we carefully stash,
And we work by the light of the moon.

Mary, Mary

Mary, Mary, quite contrary,
How does your garden grow?
"I live with my brat in a high-rise flat,
So how in the world would I know."

Hansel and Gretel

Mum said to Dad, "Those kids of ours!
The food that each of them devours!
That Hansel! Cripes, that little tick!
To watch him eat, it makes me sick!
And as for ghastly greedy Gretel –
I'm turning round to boil the kettle
And while I'm at it she's been able
To guzzle all that's on the table!"
The father merely shrugged and sighed.
Mum waved her frying-pan and cried,
"My motto is that *we* come first,
Them kids should *always* get the worst.
Now look, if we could rub them out,
There'd be more beans and sauerkraut
And stuff for you and me to eat.
Mind you, we'd have to be discreet."
The father said, "Well, what's to do?
We can't just flush them down the loo."
To which the mother answered, "No,
They're much too big. They wouldn't go."
"What if", the father said, "they fell,
Quite accidentally, down the well?"
"Oh no," Mum said, "I doubt we oughta,
It might pollute the drinkin' water.
I think it's better, on the whole,
To take them for a little stroll

And lose them in among the trees.
Now surely that's a better wheeze?"
"Let's do it!" Dad cried out. "And then
We'll never see the pigs again!"

"Walkies!" the parents cried. "It's spring!
Let's go and hear the birdies sing!
Let's look for robins in the trees!
Let's pick some wild anemones!"
Now Hansel suddenly espies
His mother's shrewd and shifty eves.
He whispers softly, "Listen, Sis,
I don't much like the smell of this.
I think our loving Mum and Dad
Are plotting something rather bad.
I think I'd better mark our track
To help us on the journey back."
So on the walk, when outward bound,
He scatters breadcrumbs on the ground.
They walk, all four, for hours and hours,
They see no robins, pick no flowers.
The wood is dark and cold and bare,
And Dad says, "Children, stay right here,
Your Mum and I have things to do.
We'll see you later, toodle-oo."
They sidled off with perfect ease
And disappeared among the trees.
"They're going to dump us!" Gretel cried.
"They won't succeed," the boy replied.
"We'll get back home, we cannot fail,
By following the breadcrumb trail.
Just take my hand and come with me,

We'll find our way, you wait and see."
But oh! Alas! Where crumbs had been
There now was nothing to be seen.
Young Gretel cried, "You silly twit,
The crows have eaten every bit."

Poor little children all alone,
The foul and filthy parents flown.
Poor little children all forlorn
To face the dismal murky morn.
"We'll starve to death!" young Hansel cried,
When all at once the youth espied
A funny little snow-white bird
Who spoke as follows, word for word:
"Come follow me, you troubled things,
I'll take you on my silver wings
To safety, to a lovely place
Where you can live in peace and grace!"

This wondrous bird then led them forth
For miles and miles towards the north
Until at last there hove in sight
A lovely cottage painted white,

And there before the cottage door
These two enraptured children saw
A sweet old dame with rosy skin
Who smiled and said, "Oh, do come in.
You must be hungry, little lambs."
She fed them treacle tarts and hams
And sugar-buns and gorgeous jam.
The children cried, "Oh, thank you, ma'am!"
The woman with the rosy cheeks
Now smiles again and softly speaks:
"My darling children, as you see,
You eat extremely well with me."

She then serves up the second treat,
A very curious roast of meat,
All sizzling hot and crispy brown.
The happy children wolf it down.
The hostess says, "Do have some more.
I doubt you've tasted this before."
Young Hansel asks her, "Is it lamb?
Or is it beef or is it ham?
Whate'er it is, I must admit
It's awfully tender, isn't it?"
The woman said, "This special meat
S'the only kind I like to eat."
Then Gretel says, "I'll make a bid –
This meat is either goat or kid."
The woman says, "Well, no-o-o and yes-s-s,
I must say *kid's* a clever guess."
She smiled and chewed and chewed and smiled
And looked so innocent and mild.

As soon as they had left the table
The woman led them to a stable.
Stable? they wondered, turning pale.
The place looked like a sort of jail
With bars and bolts and horrid things
Like manacles and iron rings.
The woman said, "Go in and look,
It's such a cosy little nook."
So Hansel, wanting to explore,
Went boldly through the open door.
The woman quickly slammed it, BANG!
The bars and locks and bolts went CLANG!

"Hey, let me out!" young Hansel cried.
"You stay in there!" the dame replied.
"I'm going to feed you up a treat
Until you're fat enough to eat."
(The Brothers Grimm who wrote this story
Made it a thousand times more gory.
I've taken out the foulest scene
In order that you won't turn green.
It is beyond me how it came
To merit such enormous fame.
Did parents really, in those days,
Agree to read such gruesome plays
To little children in the night?
And did they never die of fright?
It might have been okay, who knows,
If there'd been humour in the prose.
Did I say humour? Wilhelm Grimm?
There's not a scrap of it in him.)
I'll cut the grizzly ending short,
But even so I think I ought
To tell you gently what came next.
I'll make it brief so don't be vexed.
Just when the stove is nice and hot
And water's boiling in the pot
(The pot's for boiling Hansel in,
The stove for crisping up his skin),
Young Gretel in her pinafore
Flings open wide the oven door.

"The fire is going out!" she cried.
The woman pokes her head inside
And Gretel with a springy jump
Takes aim and kicks her on the rump.
She totters forward, in she goes
Head first, and last of all her toes.
Now Gretel with a gleeful roar
Slams shut the open oven door.
The temperature inside, she sees,
Is just on four-five-o degrees,
And soon this red-hot oven heat
Gives out the smell of roasting meat.

64

The child runs fast as she is able
To open up the prison-stable.
"Hansel!" she shouts. "We're free at last!
The foul old dame is roasting fast!"
Young Hansel cried, "Oh, well done you!
Oh, what a splendid thing to do!
But then again, you must admit
You always liked to cook a bit."

Aladdin and the Magic Lamp

A very wicked old Chinese
Called Jock MacFaddin, if you please
(His father may have been a Scot,
His mother certainly was not),
Had found while snooping on the sly
A secret cave outside Shanghai.
Excitedly he peered inside,
His eyeballs popped, he jumped and cried,
"Great heaven's above! Well, I'll be dashed!
This cave is absolutely stashed
With gorgeous gleaming precious jewels!
I wonder why those Chinese fools
Have not gone in and grabbed the lot.
Cripes, what a fortune I have got!"
The cave was huge in solid rock,
And standing there, old Chinese Jock
Espied amidst the murk and damp
A most unusual little lamp.
This lamp gave out a lovely glow
And Jock MacFaddin wasn't slow
To realise that this must be
The magic lamp that nobody
For centuries had ever found
Although they knew it was around.
Just say the word, this lamp would bring
You absolutely anything –

A ton of sweets, a dozen hams,
Full marks in end-of-term exams,
A catapult, a huge cigar,
A snazzy scarlet racing-car.
Right now Jock's mind was going through
The things he'd ask the lamp to do.
He'd turn his landlord, Kung Egg Nog,
Into an ugly jumping frog.
He'd have the Emperor O No Go
Incinerated nice and slow,
And as for Mister How U Pong
Who always beat him at mah-jong,
He'd see that Mister How U paid
In every single game they played.
And now this Scottish-Chinese knave
Moved softly through the murky cave.
Over the pearls and gold he stepped
And on towards the lamp he crept,
And just as he reached out a hand
To grab it quickly off its stand
A ghoulish snarling ghastly sound
Came up from somewhere underground,
Then slimy tendrils tugged his coat
And tried to fasten round his throat.
An icy wind swept through the cave,
Then darkness darker than the grave,
And now a voice was heard to shout,
"Get out, you filthy thief, get out!
No half-Chinese half-Scottish scamp
Is going to steal this magic lamp!"
Jock's liver and his gizzards froze,
Two bony fingers tweaked his nose.

He screamed, he ran with all his power
And did not stop for half an hour.
"Although I want that lamp!" he cried,
"I'm never going back inside!
Not gold or silver or champagne
Will get me in that cave again!"
But even now, though out of breath
And tired and frightened near to death,
This wicked half-baked mandarin
Was not too keen on giving in.

So finally, like all great thinkers
Who also happen to be stinkers,
He hit upon that ancient creed,
The changeless motto of his breed:
"*Why not get someone else to do
Your dangerous dirty work for you.*"

He hurried to the market-place
And picked him out a friendly face,
A boy who stood there trying to hawk
A load of sweet and sour pork.
Jock now behaved, to be exact,
Precisely as car-salesmen act.
He grinned and grabbed the youthful hand
And shouted, "Oh, how great! How grand!
I've found my relative at last!

My long-lost nephew from the past!"
The boy exclaimed, "My dear old trout,
I don't know *what* you're on about."
"No no!" cried this old Scots carbuncle,
"I swear that I'm your long-lost uncle.
Tell me your name. Mine's Jock MacFaddin."
The boy replied, "My name's Aladdin."
Jock said, "I'll give you seven yen,
I might go up as high as ten,
If you will help with something small.
I am your uncle after all."
The boy said, "Uncle! Oh my hat!
I'm dashed if I'm believing that.
You don't look any more Chinese
Than chalk looks like a Stilton cheese."
Jock said, "I'll raise my offer then,
I'll go as high as twenty yen."
The poor boy cried, "You tempt me so!
Oh gosh, all right then, off we go!"

So when they reached the mighty cave
Jock said, "You must be swift and brave,
Don't pause or stop for anyone,
Just grab that lamp and out you run."
"I don't quite see," Aladdin said,
"Why *you* can't get the lamp instead."
Jock cried, "Aladdin, little love
(Giving the boy a good old shove),
Inside that cave is paradise,
It's full of everything that's nice
Like bags of sweets and chocolate bars,
There's Aeros, Kit-Kats, Crunchies, Mars!"

Aladdin said, "I still don't know
Why *you* are not so keen to go."
"I'm old," Jock answered. "All that damp
Will give me rheumatism and cramp."
Aladdin said, "What if I meet
Some brute that thinks I'm good to eat?
A Gorgon or a Hippogriff?
A Doodlewhang, a Boodlesniff?
There's lots of dangerous things around
In murky caverns underground."
Jock whispered lecherous and low,
"Now, if you *really* want to know,
The only dangerous things down there
Are dancing-girls with bottoms bare.
I think you might enjoy a fling
With some curvaceous little thing."
Aladdin yelled, "That's what I crave!"
And shot into the giant cave.

Inside the cave – The gilt! The chrome!
Oh, what a mighty pleasure dome!
A cavern measureless to man!
Just like it was with Kubla Khan!
Aladdin saw the jewels and pearls,
But *where* were all the dancing-girls?
Just then he spied the little lamp
And thought, I wonder why that scamp
So badly wanted me to snatch
That thing for him. Now what's the catch?

He touched it gingerly and WHAM
There was the most almighty BANG
And suddenly in clouds of smoke
Appeared the most amazing bloke,
A sort of genie or a djinn,
An ugly brute with scarlet skin
And purple tassels in his hair
And nothing on but underwear.
The bloke cried, "I'm your magic djinn,
Feel free to ask me anything!
Just make a wish, I beg of you,
And I will make your wish come true!"
Aladdin said, a trifle comic,
"If you're the djinn then where's the tonic?"
The djinn yelled with a mighty shout,
"You think I'm joking! Try me out!"
Aladdin said, "Oh mighty djinn,
Although my hopes are pretty thin,
My only wish, I tell you true,
Is to become a djinn like you!"
The djinn was stunned. He couldn't speak.
At last he said, "You've got some cheek!
I've never heard, I'm pretty sure,
A crazy wish like that before.
This isn't just the sort of job
That can be done by any slob."
Aladdin cried, "Believe you me,
I promise you I want to be
A magic disappearing djinn
Who disappears both out and in.
I want a little lamp like yours.
I want to go to distant shores.

I want to say to anyone,
'Just make a wish,' and then it's done!"
The djinn cried, "Right! Farewell! Be brave!"
A vast explosion filled the cave,
Then thunder roared and lightning flashed
And walls caved in and ceilings crashed!

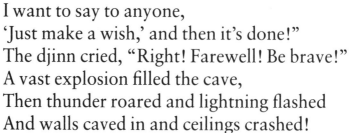

Aladdin felt as though his belly
Was being filled with boiling jelly,
As if his blood was being dried,
As though his flesh was being fried,
As if his body and his soul
Were cooking in a casserole,
As if the whole of him, no less,
Was in a mighty trouser-press,
His nails, his teeth, his bones, his skin
Were being squished and squashed so thin,
Until, just like a wind-blown feather,
He disappeared altogether.

Aladdin of the Magic Lamp
Had gone into the other camp,
He had become a mighty djinn,
A wondrous being who could spin
Around the world in half a shake
Dispensing magic in his wake.

That happened, I will have you know,
At least five hundred years ago.
He's still around and when he can
He picks upon some lucky man.
The lamp is touched, a wish expressed,
Aladdin simply does the rest,
And greatness dazzling as the sun
Then falls upon the lucky one.
He once allowed an English scamp
To touch and rub his magic lamp.
The man said, "Oh I beg, I pray,
Please help me with this lousy play.
I'm finding it extremely hard,
This struggle to become a bard."
Aladdin helped him with the plot.
Will Shakespeare murmured, "Thanks a lot."

Another time a little child
Who was no more than four or five
Said, "Help me please compose some bars
Of music that will reach the stars."
Aladdin took his hand and said,
"I'll sprinkle star-dust on your head."
All sorts of symphonies and things
Came pouring out on silver wings.
Aladdin's lamp had made him play,
And Wolfgang Mozart cried, "Hooray!"

This sort of marvellous magic wheeze
S'been going on for centuries.
Aladdin suddenly appears
(Not more than once in fifty years)
But when he does, oh boy, oh then
Great genius is born again.

Just think, next time he passes through,
The lucky person might be you.